Dinosaur Secrets REVEALED!

How High-Tech Tools Spark Discoveries

Sandra Markle

Millbrook Press / Minneapolis

For Mary Valuck and all the children at University Park Elementary School in Dallas, Texas

The author would like to thank the following people for sharing their enthusiasm and expertise: Dr. Caleb Brown, Royal Tyrrell Museum of Palaeontology, Drumheller, Alberta, Canada; Dr. Kimberley Chapelle, University of the Witwatersrand, Johannesburg, South Africa, and Stony Brook University, Stony Brook, New York; Dr. Gregory M. Erickson, Florida State University, Tallahassee, Florida; Dr. Vincent Fernandez, European Synchrotron Radiation Facility, Grenoble, France; Dr. Andréas Jannel, University of Queensland, St. Lucia, Queensland, Australia; Dr. Eric Kappus, Southwest University, El Paso, Texas; Thomas Kaye, Foundation for Scientific Advancement, Sierra Vista, Arizona; Pasha van Bijlert, PhD candidate at Utrecht University, Utrecht, the Netherlands.

A special thank-you to Skip Jeffery for his loving support during the creative process.

Millbrook Press™
An imprint of Lerner Publishing Group, Inc.
241 First Avenue North
Minneapolis, MN 55401 USA

For reading levels and more information, look up this title at www.lernerbooks.com.

Designed by Viet Chu.
Main body text set in Univers LT Std.
Typeface provided by Adobe Systems.

Library of Congress Cataloging-in-Publication Data

Names: Markle, Sandra author
Title: Dinosaur secrets revealed! : how high-tech tools spark discoveries / by Sandra Markle.
Description: Minneapolis : Millbrook Press, [2026] | Series: Sandra Markle's science discoveries | Includes bibliographical references and index. | Audience: Ages 9–12 | Audience: Grades 4–6 | Summary: "With the help of advanced technology, scientists are making new discoveries about dinosaurs. From pressure sensors to computer models, lidar scanning to laser-simulated fluorescence, new tools are revealing new information about these prehistoric creatures" —Provided by publisher.
Identifiers: LCCN 2024058384 (print) | LCCN 2024058385 (ebook) | ISBN 9798765671993 lib. bdg. | ISBN 9798765682654 epub
Subjects: LCSH: Paleontology—Technological innovations—Juvenile literature | Dinosaurs—Anatomy—Juvenile literature | Dinosaurs—Behavior—Juvenile literature
Classification: LCC QE861.5 .M34278 2026 (print) | LCC QE861.5 (ebook) | DDC 567.9—dc23/eng/20250331

LC record available at https://lccn.loc.gov/2024058384
LC ebook record available at https://lccn.loc.gov/2024058385

Manufactured in the United States of America
1-1012019-54301-5/6/2025

Contents

ARE YOU READY TO DISCOVER DINOSAUR SECRETS?!

Imprint fossil

Since the 1800s, curious people have been investigating what dinosaurs looked like, how their bodies functioned, and how they behaved. But because dinosaurs died out millions of years before any humans were around to observe them, there's still a lot we don't know. All that remains are their fossils—body parts or eggs with the living tissue replaced by rock minerals or footprints and body impressions pressed into sediment that later became rock. Paleontologists, scientists who study dinosaur fossils, learn all they can from these. But they're limited by whatever tools are available at the time. As technology advances, new high-tech tools allow scientists to study fossils in innovative ways and make new discoveries. These tools have paleontologists thinking up new questions to ask and ways to investigate even more about dinosaurs.

Fossilized egg with embryo

Fossilized bones

Imprint fossil

What new discoveries are high-tech tools revealing in dinosaur fossils?

HOW POWERFUL WAS *T. REX*'S BITE?

Greg Erickson at Florida State University saw teeth bite holes in the pelvis or hip bone of a triceratops (tri-SERRA-tops) and thought they looked like the right shape to have been made by *Tyrannosaurus rex* (tie-RAN-oh-SAWR-us rex) teeth. He tested this possibility by pushing dental putty, the material dentists used to create molds of a person's teeth, into the bite holes. Once the putty hardened, he removed it from the pelvis revealing models of the teeth that had made the bite marks. And as he'd suspected, the model teeth matched the long banana shape of *T. rex* teeth. Next, Erickson wanted to discover just how much force an adult *T. rex* could create when its jaw snapped shut.

Artists often illustrate *Tyrannosaurus rex* about to bite. Paleontologists wondered how powerful this dinosaur's bite force was.

Greg Erickson pushed the bite stick into the alligator's mouth at the back of its jaw where the strike force of the tooth will be greatest. The metal sensors were wrapped with leather pads to protect the gator's teeth.

He knew from the research of other scientists that, like today's crocodiles and alligators, seven muscles powered *T. rex* when snapping shut its lower jaw to bite. So, first, he tested the bite force of these living predatory reptiles at the St. Augustine Alligator Farm Zoological Park in Florida. He developed a testing device for the job that he called a bite stick. It had four leather-wrapped metal load sensors attached to the tip of a long plastic pipe. When Erickson approached each test animal with the bite stick, it opened its mouth wide in its defensive ready-to-bite posture. And he triggered it to bite by pushing the load sensors against the animal's teeth at the back corner of its mouth.

Load sensors work like the sensors in bathroom scales. Those sensors compute a human's weight from the amount of pressure applied to their surface. The load sensors on the bite stick compute bite force from the amount of pressure on their surface. Erickson said, "We found crocodiles and alligators struck the load sensors right at what's called *yield strength*. So, they were biting with the most force they could generate without breaking their teeth." He assumed dinosaurs likely also bit with maximum force. It was time to figure out the bite force a *T. rex*'s jaw muscles could generate. But to do that Erickson needed to know the size—thus the power—of this dinosaur's jaw muscles.

Again, previous research by other scientists led the way. Erickson knew *T. rex*'s jaw muscles passed through tunnels in its skull. So, Erickson worked with Paul Gignac at Oklahoma State University in Stillwater, Oklahoma, to measure those muscle tunnels on one fossilized *T. rex* skull. The skull was about 5 feet (1.5 m) long and almost 3 feet (0.9 m) wide, so it belonged to a large adult. Using a special computer program designed for this task, Erickson and Gignac next created a digital model of the *T. rex*'s skull. And they added simulated jaw muscles sized to fit the skull's muscle tunnels.

This computer-generated model of a *T. rex* skull shows in red the muscles that a living dinosaur would use to snap its lower jaw shut. The size of the tunnels through the skull bones made it possible to determine the size and thus the power of those muscles.

Studies of fossilized *T. rex* skulls complete with teeth revealed they contained developing teeth. So if they bit harder than yield strength and broke their teeth, replacement teeth would grow in.

After Erickson and Gignac figured out the bite force of living crocodiles and alligators, they scaled that up using their digital model. Computer animation then simulated the model *T. rex*'s jaws biting with maximum force. Erickson reported, "That revealed an adult *Tyrannosaurus rex* likely chomped down with nearly 8,000 pounds [3,628.7 kg] of force." That's more than twice the bite force of the largest crocodiles and alligators alive today and about the weight of two small cars simultaneously slamming down on one spot.

HOW SPEEDY WAS *T. REX*?

Another secret about a *Tyrannosaurus rex* scientists have long wondered about is how fast it was. Pasha van Bijlert was studying human body movement at Vrije Universiteit Amsterdam, in the Netherlands, when he saw the *T. rex* on display at the Naturalis Biodiversity Center. He said, "I remember thinking that this dinosaur walked on two legs just like people, but *T. rex* had one thing people don't have—an almost 7-meter-long [22.9 foot] tail." That made him wonder if the dinosaur's tail affected its walking speed.

Pasha van Bijlert examined the assembled 36-foot-long [10.9 m] *T. rex* skeleton on display at the Naturalis Biodiversity Center in the Netherlands. This well-preserved dinosaur was named Trix in honor of the Netherlands' Queen Beatrix.

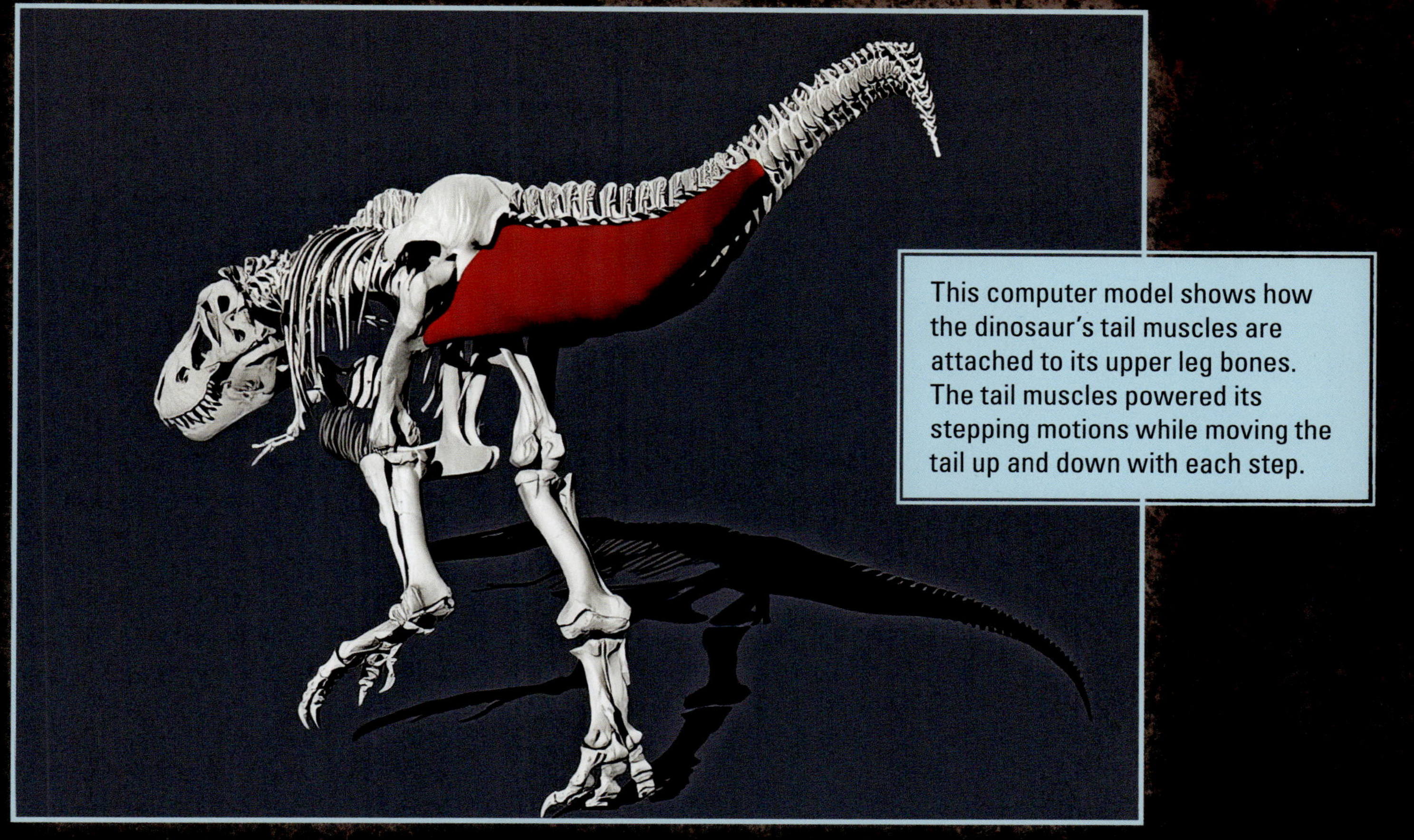

This computer model shows how the dinosaur's tail muscles are attached to its upper leg bones. The tail muscles powered its stepping motions while moving the tail up and down with each step.

Previously, researchers focused on *T. rex*'s legs while trying to estimate its speed. But van Bijlert decided to study how tail motion affected its speed. Then he would use what he learned to determine the dinosaur's possible average walking speed.

When the *T. rex* skeleton was first assembled for display, researchers scanned its bones. Using these scans, van Bijlert created a 3D computer model of the dinosaur. Next, he worked with this model to simulate how the dinosaur's tail movement powered its legs. He reported, "I estimated a walking *T. rex* would take two steps every three seconds." But to judge walking speed, van Bijlert also needed to know how far a big adult *T. rex* like Trix traveled with each step.

Based on the age of the rock formations, scientists believe the tyrannosaur tracks van Bijlert studied were made by *Albertosaurus sarcophagus*. It was a slightly smaller tyrannosaur whose fossilized bones have been found only in Alberta, Canada. Scientists believe it lived about two million years earlier than *T. rex*.

The easiest way to find out this information would have been to measure the distance between two fossilized *T. rex* footprints. Unfortunately, no such footprints have been found. So, van Bijlert used the distance between the tracks of another tyrannosaur *Albertosaurus sarcophagus* (al-BERT-oh-SAWR-us SARK-off-a-gus). And he scaled up that step distance because an adult *T. rex* was a little larger. Based on this, he predicted each of the tyrannosaur's steps covered about 6.5 feet (1.9 m). Then he used the number of steps he estimated his model dinosaur likely completed in one minute. And he multiplied that by the distance the fossilized footprint study estimated would have been covered by the adult *T. rex* in that time. The result was *T. rex*'s probable walking speed.

Van Bijlert said, "The result was the surprisingly slow speed of about 4.5 kilometers [2.8 miles] per hour." That means a *T. rex*'s walking speed was close to the average walking speed of a human. So, if a *T. rex* was around today, healthy young adults could probably walk alongside it—if they dared!

Could *T. rex* also run? Some paleontologists don't think it could due to its massive size. They suspect it was so heavy that running might have broken its leg bones. Van Bijlert doesn't believe that *T. rex* was limited to walking, and it would have had reasons to speed up. For example, when it was hunting—or running away from an even larger *T. rex*.

To investigate *T. rex*'s running speed, van Bijlert is studying emus. He believes this bird's skeletal structure and muscles are similar enough to those of dinosaurs to provide some clues. But, so far, he's still working to discover how *T. rex*'s body might have moved when it was running.

Scientists believe birds, such as these emus, are descended from dinosaurs because they have similar skeletons and reproduce by laying eggs, among other commonalities. Compare the position of the emu's legs as it runs to both previous images of tyrannosaurs in action.

DO ANY DINOSAUR FOSSILS HAVE HIDDEN PARTS?

Could there be something more to a dinosaur imprint fossil than what is immediately visible? An imprint fossil is created when a living creature is buried and decays between layers of sand or mud that become rock. Thomas Kaye, the principal investigator and director at the Foundation for Scientific Advancement in Sierra Vista, Arizona, read how bacteria viewed in laser light revealed new details that had been invisible in normal lighting. No one had tried examining imprint fossils with laser light, so he decided to see what it might reveal about dinosaur imprint fossils, such as the one of *Anchiornis huxleyi* (ANK-ee-or-nis HUX-lee-eye).

This imprint fossil of *Anchiornis huxleyi* shows the dinosaur's feathers and bones. You can also see sharp claws at the tips of its toes.

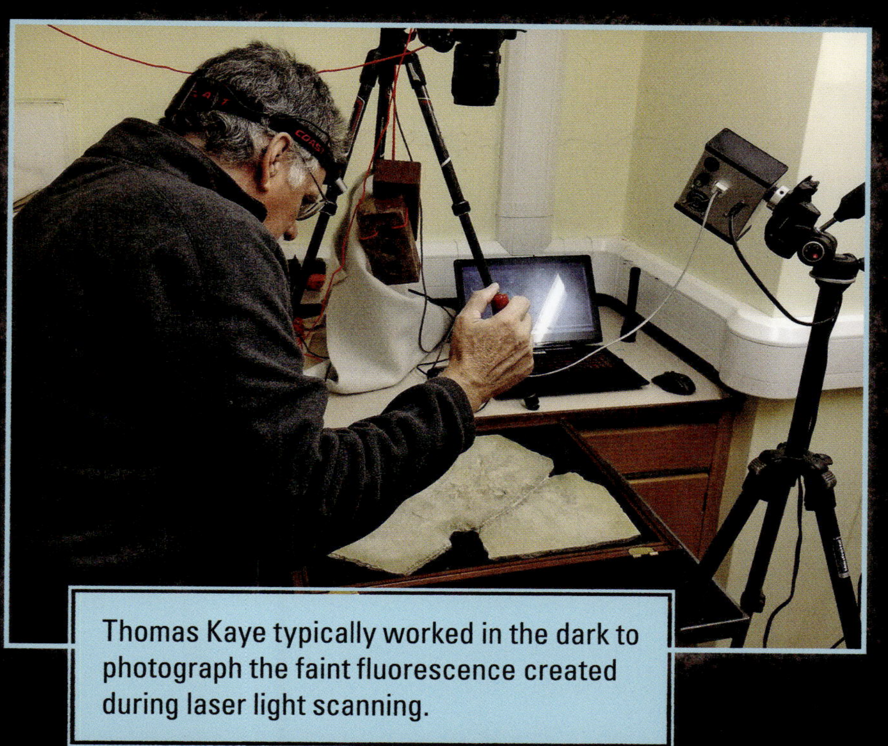

Thomas Kaye typically worked in the dark to photograph the faint fluorescence created during laser light scanning.

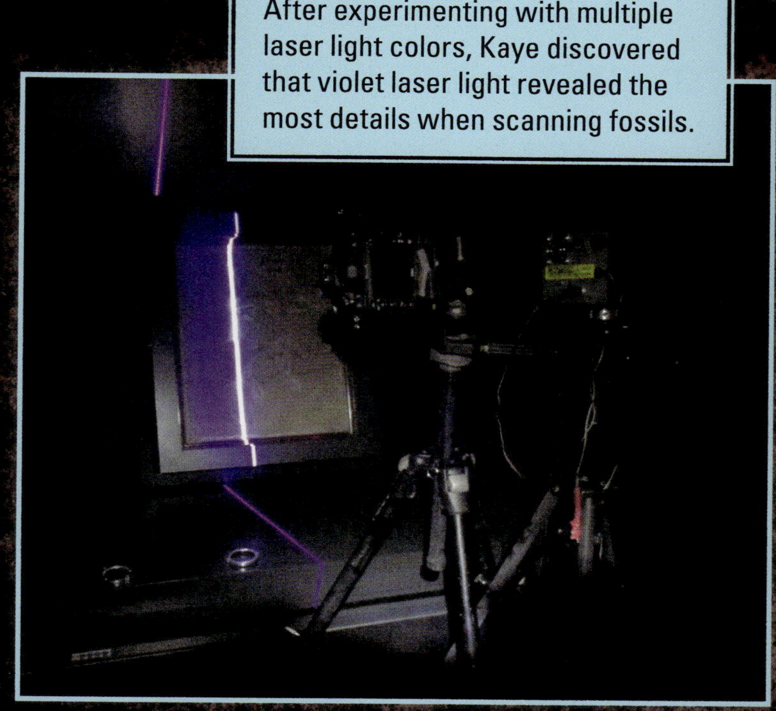

After experimenting with multiple laser light colors, Kaye discovered that violet laser light revealed the most details when scanning fossils.

The reason why laser light reveals more details is because sunshine or light from light bulbs only bounces off surfaces to reveal external features. But laser light striking a surface causes any chemicals embedded there to glow. And different chemicals glow in different colors. That can reveal details not otherwise visible. Imprint fossils form when an animal is buried and then decays. So, while the bones, feathers, teeth, and other hard parts leave clear physical impressions, the decaying soft body tissues deposit chemicals that only become visible with laser light.

Wearing goggles to protect his eyes from the laser beam's intensity, Kaye tried viewing the *Anchiornis* imprint fossil illuminated with laser light. He saw some colors. That meant the laser was stimulating chemicals in the fossil, making previously invisible parts glow enough to become visible. Then Kaye photographed the laser illuminated imprint fossil with a digital camera to study the image.

Kaye and fellow researcher Michael Pittman used laser-stimulated fluorescence to study the *Anchiornis* imprint fossil at the Shandong Tianyu Museum of Nature in Shandong, China.

In normal light

In laser light

Chemical tests of the pigments, natural coloring materials, found on the imprinted outline of feathers of this *Anchiornis* fossil revealed it had black-and-white wings, a dark body, and a rust-red head crest.

From studies of the *Anchiornis* imprint fossil illuminated with normal light, paleontologists described it as being chicken-sized with winglike front legs. They could see that its leg feathers were too short to power flight but long enough to let it glide between locations. The impression also showed it had curved toe claws for climbing. From his laser light investigations, Kaye discovered the previously unknown fact that *Anchiornis*'s feet had bumpy skin that undoubtedly helped it grip during climbing and hold on upon landing.

After nearly a decade of using laser-stimulated fluorescence to study different dinosaur imprint fossils, Kaye is also working with a new high-tech tool. He said, "When you see a fluorescence, the color can be created by multiple chemicals. We have a new camera that takes a photo right after the laser light is turned off. So, it takes an image as the fluorescence fades." This camera will provide a chance to see even more when viewing an imprint fossil because it will show the chemical structure of the body parts that were pressed into the sediment that later became rock.

WERE BABIES DIFFERENT FROM ADULTS?

In 1976 James Kitching and his field assistant Regent "Lucas" Huma discovered a clutch, or group, of *Massospondylus carinatus* (mas-oh-SPON-di-lus CAR-i-na-tus) eggs in Golden Gate Highlands National Park in South Africa. In the late 1970s, and then again in the early 2000s, experts carefully chipped away enough rock material to reveal dinosaur embryos developing inside two of those eggs. Seeing the embryos made the scientists wonder how—other than size—these young dinosaurs were different from the adults. It took a high-tech tool, the synchrotron, to investigate.

Each *Massospondylus carinatus* embryo curled up inside its egg is 3 inches (7.6 cm) long.

Paleontologists don't know how quickly hatchlings grew up. But they know from studying the fossil remains of adult *Massospondylus* that they grew to be about 20 feet (6 m) long.

In a synchrotron, such as the European Synchrotron Radiation Facility, electrons (atomic particles with a negative charge) release energy while circulating around and around inside the giant storage ring. The result is extremely powerful X-rays—as much as millions of times more powerful than those produced by conventional X-ray machines in hospitals. The synchrotron's powerful X-rays are released in forty thin streams, called beamlines. These are directed to a series of laboratories, called hutches, where scientists place whatever will be scanned. When the X-rays reach the object, their high energy allows them to partially pass through it before being picked up by a detector. A computer processes the recorded signal to create a series of images. These are like thin slices of the scanned object.

This is the European Synchrotron Radiation Facility in Grenoble, France. It is a giant ring 2,769 feet (844 m) around, and it provides high-powered X-ray beams for research projects.

Paleontologist Kimberley Chapelle became curious about the *Massospondylus* embryos while studying at the University of the Witwatersrand in Johannesburg, South Africa. In 2015 she applied for and received a grant to investigate the embryos with the help of the European Synchrotron Radiation Facility. As a beamline scientist there, Vincent Fernandez assisted Chapelle with her research. Even though the one *Massospondylus* embryo being scanned was small, the extremely high-resolution scanning took almost eight hours. Next, Fernandez and Chapelle processed the scans. Fernandez explained, "We work with special 3D software, and first it is all gray values (shades of gray). Then we have to tell the computer what is bone, what is eggshell, and what is sediment. The different gray values are based on density (how compacted it is). The synchrotron is very good at picking up the fine detail contrast in the density. Next, we have the computer make the different bones different colors."

Chapelle focused on the embryo's skull. One by one, like completing a computer jigsaw puzzle, she arranged the colored bones to assemble the skull.

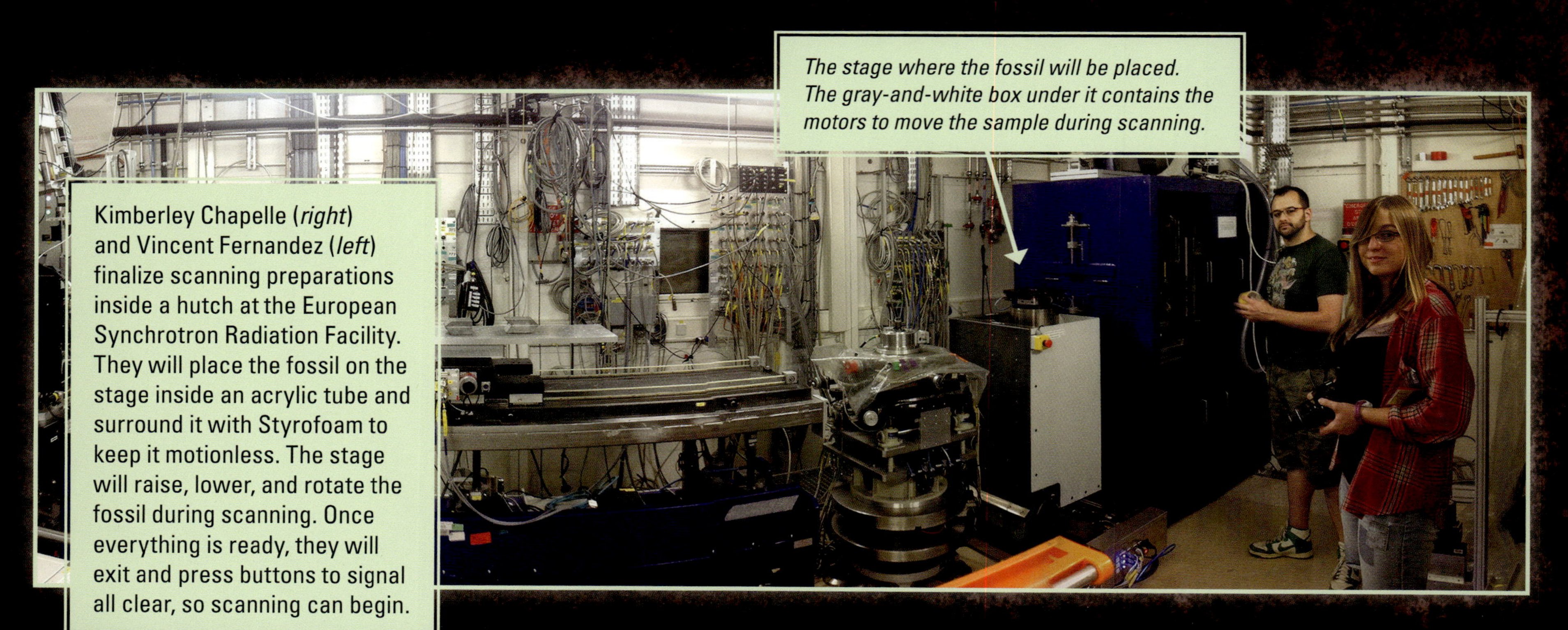

The stage where the fossil will be placed. The gray-and-white box under it contains the motors to move the sample during scanning.

Kimberley Chapelle (*right*) and Vincent Fernandez (*left*) finalize scanning preparations inside a hutch at the European Synchrotron Radiation Facility. They will place the fossil on the stage inside an acrylic tube and surround it with Styrofoam to keep it motionless. The stage will raise, lower, and rotate the fossil during scanning. Once everything is ready, they will exit and press buttons to signal all clear, so scanning can begin.

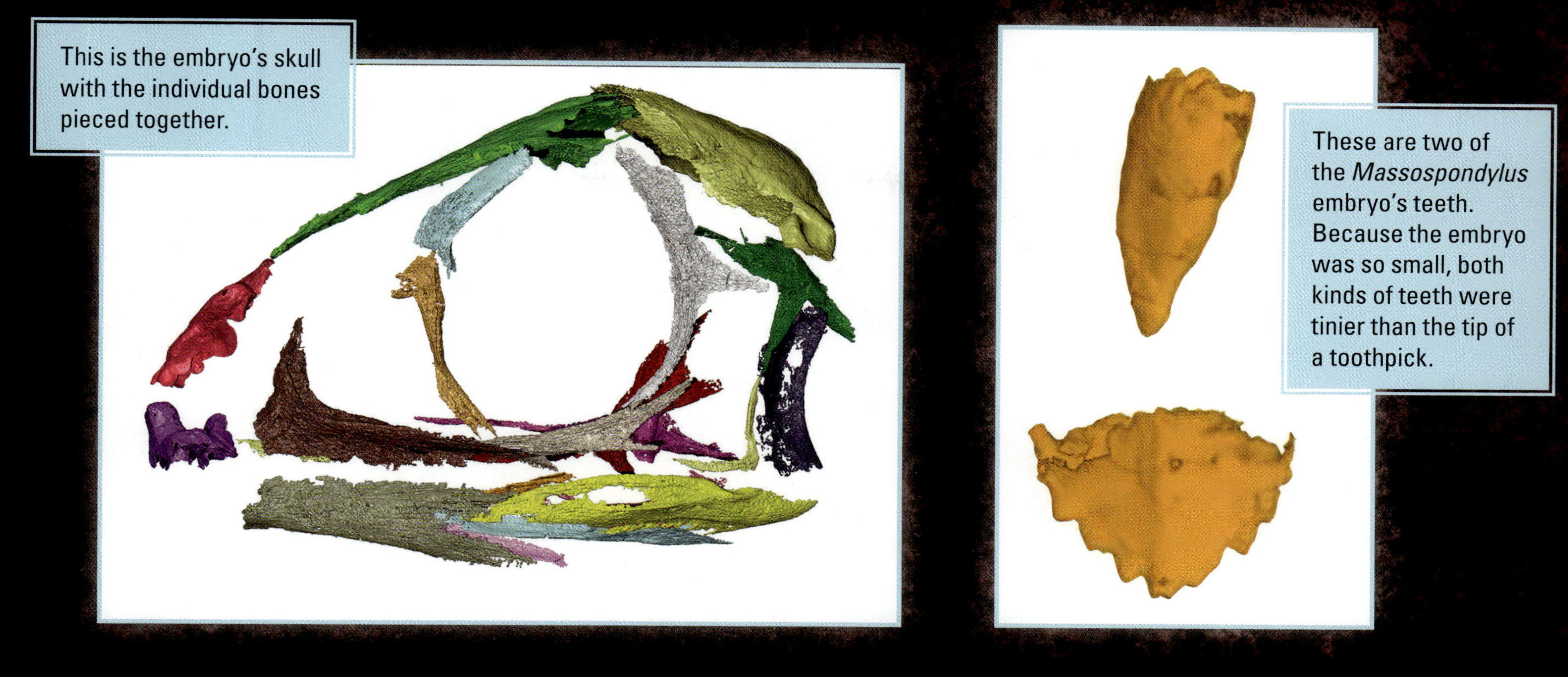

This is the embryo's skull with the individual bones pieced together.

These are two of the *Massospondylus* embryo's teeth. Because the embryo was so small, both kinds of teeth were tinier than the tip of a toothpick.

Chapelle was very excited because she saw the embryo not only had teeth, but it had two types of teeth. One set of wider and serrated teeth was very similar in shape to adult *Massospondylus* teeth. Those would be the ones the embryo hatched with. It also had simple triangular teeth that would have been resorbed (broken down) or shed before hatching. Such teeth are found in the embryos of some living animals, such as crocodiles and geckos. Finding it here was significant because this was the first time for this feature to be seen in a dinosaur embryo.

Chapelle explained, "*Massospondylus* is a really old species of dinosaur that lived over 200 million years ago. And these embryo teeth are like we find today in reptilians. Dinosaurs, crocodiles, geckos, and such are all part of a larger group of related animals. We don't know how widely distributed it is to have embryo teeth or why they exist. But the reason animals have them today is probably the reason *Massospondylus* had them in the past. So, I wonder why those dinosaur embryos had them?" And once again, a discovery raises a fresh mystery to be tackled by future investigations.

DID DINOSAURS HAVE FAMILIES?

Fossilized bones and teeth provide clues about a dinosaur's body structure, such as it having large hind legs and small front legs or it having teeth that show it was a meat eater or a plant eater. Fossilized footprints, places dinosaurs stepped in mud or sand that later became rock, don't share those kinds of details. But the shape of fossil footprints does tell something about the dinosaur's identity. For example, a three-toed footprint with a large spoon-shaped middle toe, such as the one in the photo, shows the dinosaur that made it was a type of hadrosaur (HA-druh-sawr). That is a group of large plant-eating dinosaurs that usually walked on four legs and had duckbill-like jaws.

Look at the large, fossilized dinosaur footprint next to Eric Kappus. This is at the Cerro de Cristo Rey dinosaur tracksite, an area where many fossilized dinosaur footprints have been found, near El Paso, Texas.

Eric Kappus points to the group of theropod tracks he found on a rock wall. When dinosaurs walked across this area, it was flat mud. Over time, the section became rock that was lifted and tilted.

In this photo, the footprints are outlined in red.

Fossil footprints also reveal something bones don't—insights into how a dinosaur traveled from one place to another. Fossil footprints can show if a dinosaur walked on two legs or four. The distance between footprints in a line reveals whether it was walking or running. And similar sets of tracks close together and going in the same direction indicate the dinosaur was likely part of a group. But it wasn't until 2002 that fossil footprints helped solve another mystery about dinosaurs.

Eric Kappus was a graduate student at the University of Texas at El Paso in El Paso, Texas, when he discovered a group of theropod footprints. He was on a field trip in an open-pit mine when a lumpy rock wall caught his attention. He recognized the bumps and grooves as fossilized footprints made by a theropod (THEH-ruh-paad)—a group of large, meat-eating dinosaurs that walked on two legs. Since fossilized footprints don't reveal anything more specific, he didn't know which theropod species left the prints. But it was the number of different-sized footprints close together that made him take a closer look.

Acrocanthosaurus was one of the largest theropods ever to live. Its fossil bones have been found across both the Eastern and Western United States.

Kappus said, "I first spotted two footprints. Then I saw eight or nine more. In about a 30-foot-square [2.7 sq. m] area there were bigger tracks and smaller tracks that were all the same type, closely spaced, and going in the same direction. I thought, 'Wow, this could be a family group!'" Paleontologists had long wondered if theropod adults stayed with their young after they hatched.

Kappus believed the tracks he discovered might have been made by *Acrocanthosaurus* (AK-row-KAN-thuh-SAWR-us) since its fossilized bones are commonly found throughout Texas. But whatever kind of theropod made the tracks, it was the spacing that was most exciting. Kappus explained, "The big theropod's footprints were not far apart—spaced as though it was walking very slowly. And crossing these were little theropod footprints. These were far apart—spaced as though the little theropod was running to keep up."

For nearly twenty years following his discovery, Kappus continued to search the open-pit mine on foot, looking for more track evidence of theropod family behavior. Eventually, he was hired as a professor at Southwest University in El Paso. One of his students was a professional surveyor and helped him expand his search using lidar (light detection and ranging) technology. Kappus could then search for fossil tracks in more rugged areas.

The lidar equipment maps an area as it repeatedly travels in back-and-forth paths similar to the way someone usually mows a lawn. The machine shoots out hundreds of thousands of laser pulses every second. The laser pulses bounce off the ground and reflect back to the machine. It records the time between when the pulses shoot out and when the bounced-back reflections are received. Later, a computer running a specialized program interprets those locations and the distance data to create a 3D map of the scanned area showing the ground's contours. That makes it possible to discover fossil tracks human eyes could miss.

Using lidar scanning, Kappus also discovered footprints left by other kinds of dinosaurs, including a type of iguanodon (ig-WHA-noh-don) that once roamed the area. Iguanodon is a group

Eric Kappus (*left*) works with surveyor Dean Van Matre (*right*). A lidar scanning device can be flown back and forth over an area on a drone or a plane. Or, as in this picture, it can be fixed to a tripod and moved to scan the ground one section at a time.

Computer software transformed the data from the lidar scan into a 3D map to reveal dinosaur tracks by showing shallower areas as yellow, deeper areas as green, and the deepest areas as blue. This image shows an iguanodon footprint.

Paleontologists discovered dinosaur fossilized eggs arranged in what were clearly nest sites. At some, they also found fossilized theropod footprints.

of different kinds of large, plant-eating dinosaurs that usually walked on four legs and had back legs that were longer than the front legs. The color contoured image the computer made of the footprint revealed that it was quite deep. That indicated the ground was soft when the iguanodon walked there.

Kappus has yet to find any additional evidence of theropod family behavior. He continues to search, though. And he remains hopeful the lidar technology will deliver that supporting proof. Meanwhile, his discovery has other scientists taking a fresh look at fossil dinosaur nest sites where theropod tracks were found. Previously, these were believed to be the footprints of meat eaters stealing eggs to eat. Kappus said, "Now they think maybe the adults stayed around to protect the nests and teach the young to hunt."

HOW DID GIANTS WALK WITHOUT BREAKING THEIR FEET?

Among the largest dinosaurs to leave fossilized footprints were sauropods (SAW-ruh-paadz)—a group of very big plant-eating dinosaurs with long necks, long tails, and four pillarlike legs. Since many were giants from 50 feet (15.2 m) to over 100 feet (30.4 m) long, they left huge footprints, such as the ones discovered in 2016 on Dampier Peninsula in Western Australia. Each of these averaged 5 feet 9 inches (1.7 m) in diameter. Paleontologists thought such large dinosaurs were heavy enough that they needed to remain partly submerged so water helped to support their bodies. They were shocked to find giant sauropod footprints where the rock was a mix of sandstone and mudstone, indicating it was likely dry land when the dinosaurs walked across it. Andréas Jannel saw some of those giant dinosaur footprints while studying at the University of Queensland in Australia. He said, "I wondered, 'How did such a big sauropod walk on land without its bodyweight breaking its foot bones?'"

Andréas Jannel near a footprint left long ago by a giant sauropod

From fossilized bones discovered in Australia, scientists estimate that the sauropod *Rhoetosaurus brownei* was as much as 49 feet (14.9 m) long. Some scientists believe sauropods could rear up briefly on their back legs and, using their tail for support, grab mouthfuls of leaves from tall trees.

Jannel considered how he might tackle this dinosaur mystery. Then, to his surprise, he learned that 120 years earlier paleontologists had already proposed a possible solution. Though no individual was credited with the idea, it stated that sauropods walked without breaking the bones in their feet because they had a giant, soft-tissue footpad. It was suggested that it worked similar to the way an elephant's footpad directs the load of its weight away from the foot bones. Long ago, no technology was available for testing this proposed explanation. Jannel was intrigued by the idea because he had high-tech tools available to conduct the necessary research and find out if it was correct.

He focused on one of the best-known sauropods whose fossil bones were commonly found in Australia: *Rhoetosaurus brownei* (REET-oh-sawr-us BROWN-ay). First, he took pictures of all the surfaces of the bones making up

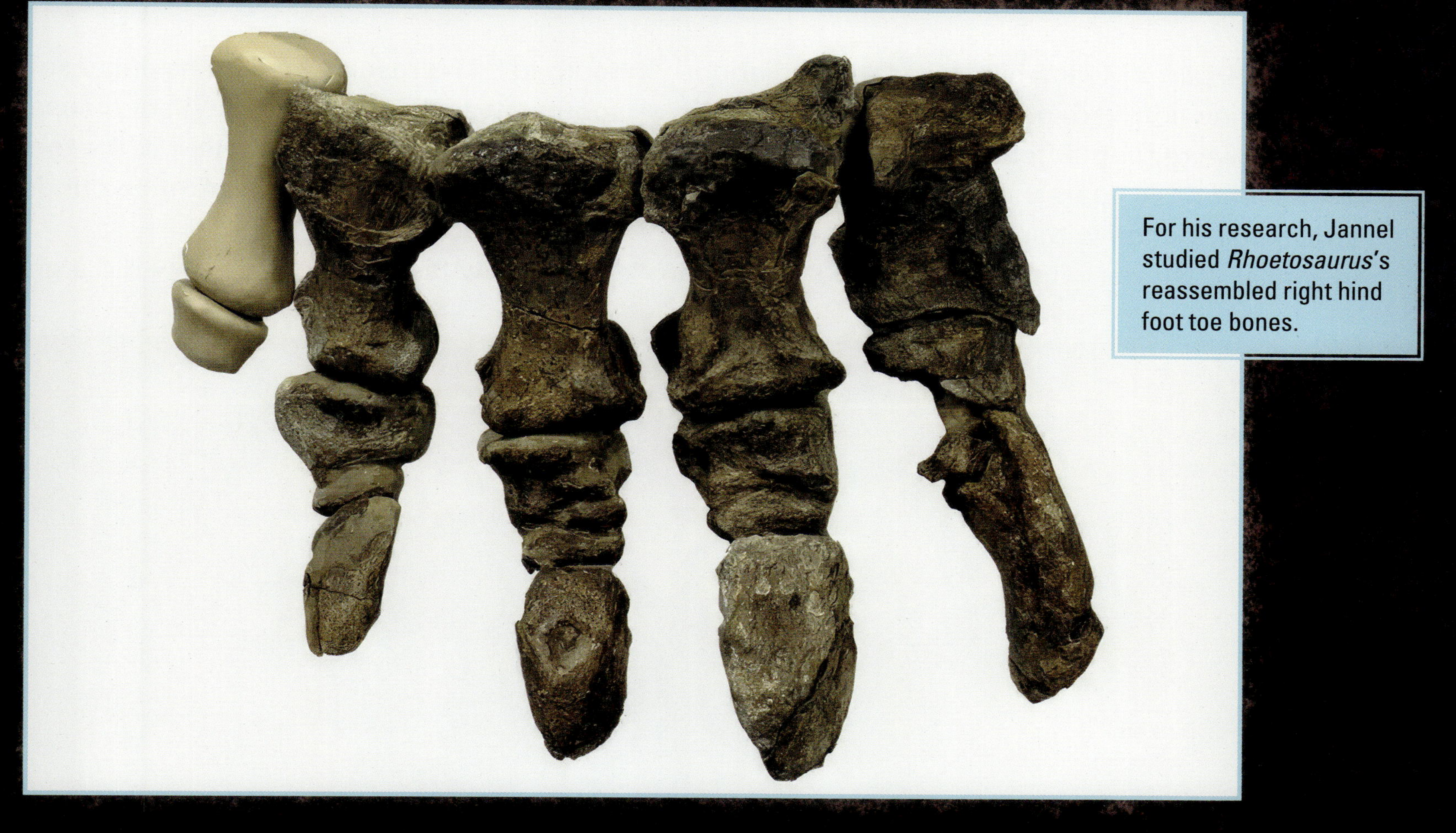

For his research, Jannel studied *Rhoetosaurus*'s reassembled right hind foot toe bones.

its reconstructed right hind foot. Next, he used computer software to create a 3D model of that foot. He reported, "Using software that is usually used for animation, I easily moved the bones—something that would have been difficult with life-sized model bones." The 3D computer model let Jannel compare how the toe bones would have been positioned as the sauropod's foot moved, adjusting to different body postures. And he could compare how those toe bones would be positioned while walking, with and without a soft-tissue footpad.

Jannel said, "Meanwhile, I was reading about engineering software used to test the stress of loading [weight] on different parts of bridges. So, I spent three years using that software to test stress distribution within the sauropod toe bones in similar postures with and without a soft-tissue footpad." The results showed having a soft-tissue footpad was the only way the giant dinosaur could have stood on dry land. Without it, the toe bones would have broken or even crumbled under its immense bodyweight.

But how fast—or how slowly—did a giant

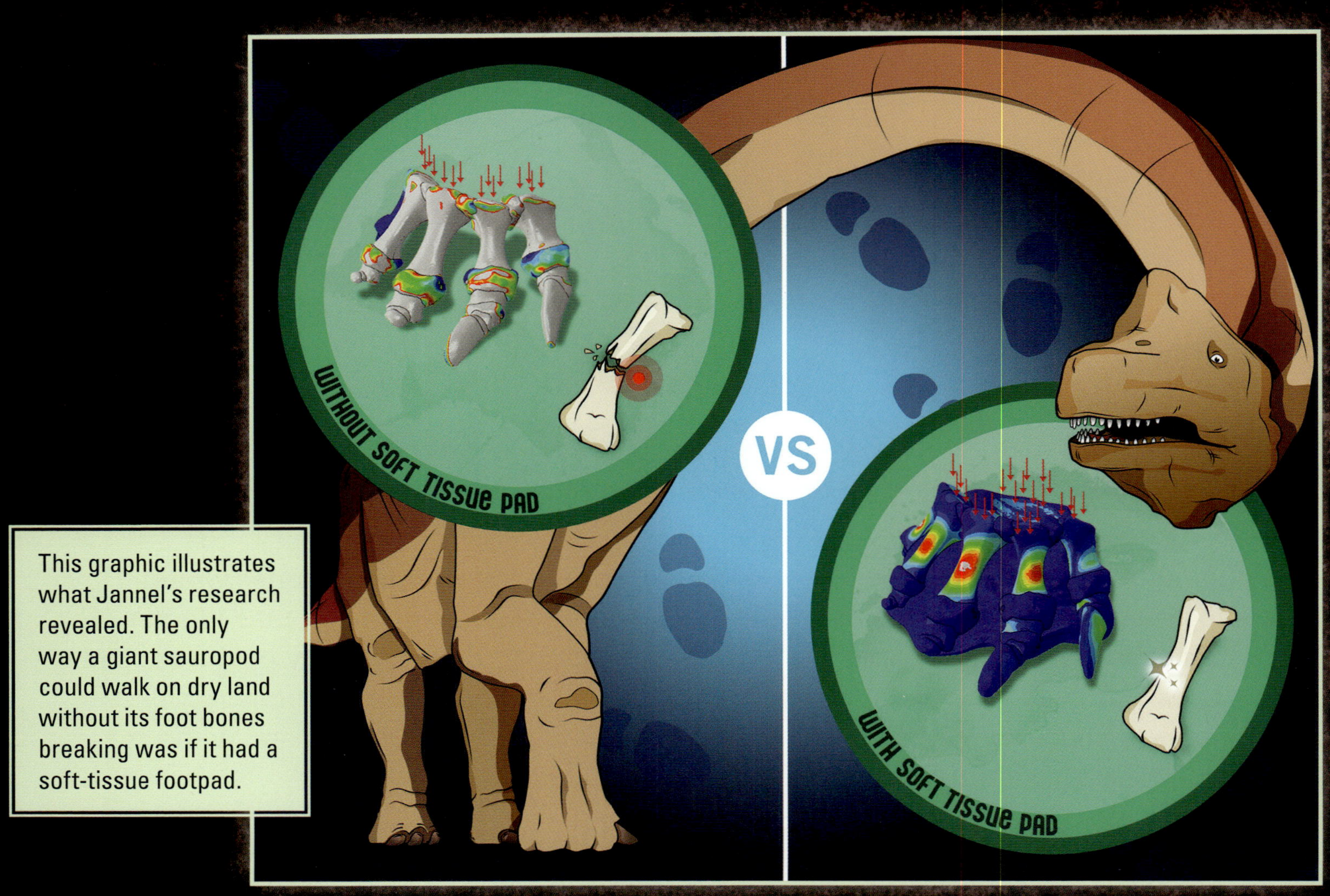

This graphic illustrates what Jannel's research revealed. The only way a giant sauropod could walk on dry land without its foot bones breaking was if it had a soft-tissue footpad.

Argentinosaurus was among the largest known sauropods at an estimated 121 feet (36.8 m) long and weighing 22,000 pounds (9,979 kg). Footprints show *Argentinosaurus* traveled in groups accompanied by smaller dinosaurs.

sauropod walk? Jannel said, "It's tricky to answer that. I think a sauropod could only move one of its four feet at a time to keep from tipping over. But to know that for certain or to estimate its walking speed we need a couple of sets of tracks showing back foot and front footprints from one individual. Since sauropods traveled in groups, here in the Dampier Peninsula in Western Australia, we are still trying to isolate sets of tracks in the middle of thousands."

Paleontologists are flying drones carrying lidar equipment to scan large areas, and computer software is transforming the results to reveal footprints. But the effort to isolate the needed individual track set is ongoing. For now, how fast it walked remains unknown.

WHAT CAN BE LEARNED FROM A SUPER WELL-PRESERVED DINOSAUR?

What if you didn't need to imagine how a dinosaur looked when it was alive? What if you found a fossil that let you see its body complete with skin and spiky armor? That happened in 2011 when Shawn Funk, a heavy equipment operator at the Suncor Millennium Mine in Alberta, Canada, dug into oil sands there. The dinosaur's features weren't immediately visible, however, because the fossil was encased in a hard, concrete-like material.

This dinosaur fossil is made up of several broken pieces placed together. But it is still so lifelike that it appears to be sleeping.

Although an attempt was made to find all of this fossil, only the front half of the dinosaur was recovered. Following completion of the excavation, Mark Mitchell, with a little help from other technicians, spent six years carefully removing the concrete coating to prepare the fossil for study.

All fossils found in Alberta belong to the province and go to museums. This one went to the Royal Tyrrell Museum of Paleontology. There, Caleb Brown, a paleontologist and member of the museum's research team, led studies of the fossilized dinosaur's body shape and features. Then, based on the dinosaur's narrow skull, the sutures (immovable joints) on top of its skull, and shoulder spines, the team concluded this was a nodosaur (NOH-doe-sor). This plant-eating, land-roaming, armored dinosaur is similar to an ankylosaur (AN-kee-low-sor) but without a club-tipped tail.

The research team also found enough details about this dinosaur that were different from any other nodosaur already discovered to designate it as a new species, or kind, of nodosaur. They named it *Borealopelta markmitchelli* (bor-EE-al-oh-pell-tah MARK-MITCH-ell-eye). *Borealo* means "northern" in Latin and refers to the region where the fossil was found; *pelta* refers to an ancient type of shield and identifies it as a type of nodosaur. Finally, *markmitchelli* honors the technician who worked hard to expose the dinosaur's features. Brown said, "It's the Mona Lisa of fossils—not just bones but a dinosaur as it would have been." So, what could this incredibly well-preserved fossil reveal about the living *Borealopelta*?

The museum team also discovered that skin was still on the fossil. But as a result of fossilization, it became a black carbon coating. They were hopeful some of the original organelles, parts of cells, remained. They first tried looking at this material with a scanning electron microscope, a very high-powered microscope that magnifies a sample as much as five hundred thousand times. Brown reported, "We couldn't see anything useful. Ten years ago, we would have said most of the living material is gone. But now we know that isn't necessarily true. And there is a second approach, which is to examine the fossil's carbon coating from a chemical standpoint with a mass spectrometer."

Jakob Vinther at the University of Bristol performed the mass spectrometer study of

These are closely spaced rows of small armor plates on the back and sides of *Borealopelta*. Its armor also included spike-shaped plates and a pair of long spines—one on each shoulder. All of these were covered with sheaths of keratin—the same material as human fingernails.

Based on the portion of the fossilized *Borealopelta*'s body recovered, the living dinosaur was about 18 feet (5.4 m) long and weighed around 3,000 pounds (1,360.7 kg).

Borealopelta's skin sample. This device converts material into a gas and analyzes it to determine the chemical makeup. Although the first mass spectrometer was built in 1912, it took years of technological advances to produce modern high-tech mass spectrometers that can detect the chemicals in fossil material. Vinther's study of *Borealopelta*'s skin sample revealed an abundance of the same chemical that gives people and animals reddish hair.

Brown reported, "We can say *Borealopelta* was a reddish-brown color. We don't know how extreme the shade of red was or if it was striped, spotted, or had other colors involved." By performing further studies of the coloring matter in *Borealopelta*'s skin, Brown and the team determined the dinosaur was very dark on its back and very light on its belly. Such shading is also common in modern animals. It allows them to blend into their surroundings and hide from predators.

Because of its stomach contents, scientists wondered if *Borealopelta* preferred dining on ferns.

With the back half of *Borealopelta* missing, the dinosaur's stomach was exposed, revealing the fossilized remains of its last meal. Brown and the museum team examined this and discovered that the plant-eating dinosaur had eaten a lot of ferns and a small amount of palmlike plant parts as well as some conifer needles. They wondered if that meant *Borealopelta* mainly ate ferns or if that was what was available. Of course, there was no way to know the answer from this one meal.

Borealopelta's stomach contents also included rounded, pea- to grape-sized objects. Those are gastroliths, rocks that some animals—both in prehistoric and modern times—swallow to help their stomach grind up what they eat. Brown said, "We want to study those [gastroliths] because *Borealopelta* wasn't found where it [likely] lived. We know that because it was found in sediment determined to have been at the bottom of a prehistoric sea. So, if those rocks in its gut are only found in a certain area, we might learn [the area on land] where the dinosaur came from."

Along with further research on the gastroliths, Brown is collaborating with a specialist to generate a 3D computer model of *Borealopelta*. It will be animated to study how the individual armor plates might have moved to shield the dinosaur's internal organs from a predator's bite or a rival *Borealopelta*'s shove. Brown said, "I'm hopeful that will reveal which of those two interactions was the main reason it had its body armor."

In addition to plant material and gastroliths, *Borealopelta*'s stomach contained charcoal, leading the scientists to believe it was feeding in a recently burned area.

ARE YOU READY TO DISCOVER *MORE* DINOSAUR SECRETS

High-tech tools have made it possible for paleontologists to investigate fossils in new ways and reveal some amazing information about dinosaurs. But did you notice that some discoveries led to more questions and additional mysteries to investigate? That's exciting!

Fictional stories usually have definite endings. But real-life science stories, such as the ones you've just explored, often end with a cliffhanger and the question, *What's next?* A new generation of scientists and engineers is already improving existing equipment and developing new high-tech tools. And a new generation of paleontologists is putting these to work as they ask new questions about prehistoric animals. Who knows what secrets will one day be revealed to help us better understand all those incredible, fascinating dinosaurs.

Did *T. rex* protect its young and train them to hunt? That is one of the many facts paleontologists are still working to reveal.

A Note from Sandra Markle

Dinosaurs are exciting creatures that grab our imagination. I've spent twenty years writing magazine articles and books about dinosaurs. This gave me opportunities to talk with paleontologists from around the world about their fieldwork exploring, discovering, and unearthing dinosaur fossils.

Recently, I read about how new high-tech tools were enabling paleontologists to make new discoveries in laboratories as well as in the field. I was intrigued! That launched me into interviewing the experts you've met in this book. I'm honored to share their research, the amazing discoveries they've made, and the challenges they inspire for future research. Perhaps the best thing about dinosaurs is that they keep us looking for new ways to reveal their secrets.

What Made Dinosaurs Different from Other Animals?

Scientists describe dinosaurs as part of a group of egg-laying reptiles that lived long ago. But they were also distinct from crocodilians, which were other reptiles living alongside them and includes today's reptiles, such as alligators. A dinosaur had two holes in its skull—one behind each eye socket—that crocodilians lacked. Large, strong jaw muscles stretched through those holes and attached to the top of the skull, letting a dinosaur's jaw shut with powerful bite force. Also, a dinosaur's body structure put its legs directly below its hips, letting it lift its belly completely off the ground. This let it walk and run more easily and with less expended energy than the sprawling leg gait of crocodilians.

T. rex skull

Alligator skull

Dino Data

Discover key facts about each of the featured dinosaurs based on studies of their fossils.

Acrocanthosaurus
fossil found in the United States
Size: 38 feet (11.5 m) long
Weight: 6 tons (5.4 t)
Teeth and diet: Thin, curved, inward-slanting teeth; likely mainly ate other dinosaurs
Locomotion: Walked on two legs
Habitat: Dry areas
Special feature: Sixty-eight teeth with serrated (jagged) edges

Anchiornis huxleyi
fossil found in China
Size: 24 inches (60.9 cm) long with a wingspan of 1.8 feet (57.4 cm)
Weight: 2.2 pounds (1 kg)
Teeth and diet: Tiny sharp teeth lining beaklike mouth; likely mainly ate insects and lizards
Locomotion: Climbed trees using long, curved claws and spread feathered limbs for gliding flight
Habitat: Forests
Special feature: A long tail that helped it steer and stay balanced while gliding

Borealopelta markmitchelli
fossil found in Canada
Size: 18 feet (5.5 m) long
Weight: 3,000 pounds (1,360.7 kg)
Teeth and diet: Small, flat teeth; ate plants
Locomotion: Walked on four legs
Habitat: Forests and fern meadows
Special feature: A 20-inch-long (51 cm) swordlike backward projecting spine on each shoulder

Massospondylus carinatus
fossils found in South Africa, Zimbabwe, Botswana, and Lesotho
Size: 20 feet (6 m) long
Weight: 2,200 pounds (997.9 kg)
Teeth and diet: Pointed front teeth and spatula-shaped back teeth; ate plants
Locomotion: Walked on two legs with the back legs longer than the front legs
Habitat: Dry environment
Special feature: Sharp thumb claw on each front foot

Rhoetosaurus brownei
fossils found in Australia
Size: 49 feet (14.9 m) long
Weight: 19,841 pounds (8,999.7 kg)
Teeth and diet: Narrow, flat teeth; ate plants
Locomotion: Walked on four legs
Habitat: Wet, warm forests
Special feature: A very long neck

Tyrannosaurus rex
fossils found in the United States and Canada
Size: 42 feet (12.8 m) long
Weight: 1,600 pounds (725 kg)
Teeth and diet: Large, conical, serrated-edged teeth; mainly ate other dinosaurs
Locomotion: Walked on two legs
Habitat: Forests, near rivers, and in open areas
Special feature: Large wide-set eyes

Timeline

The featured dinosaurs did not all live at the same time. Check out when each of the featured dinosaurs lived during what is called the Age of Dinosaurs.

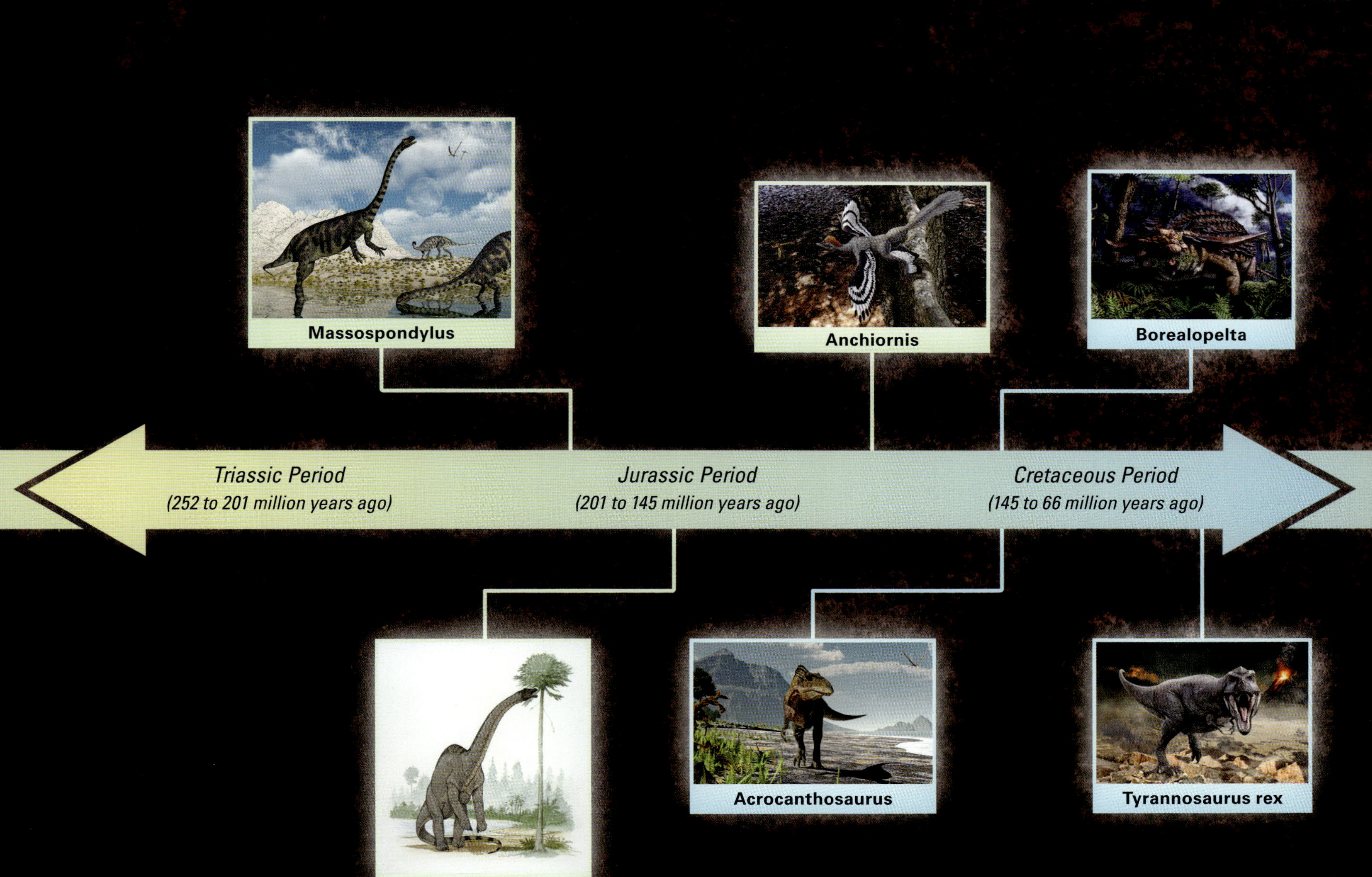

Glossary

adult: fully developed individual able to reproduce

ankylosaur: an armored, plant-eating dinosaur with a club-tipped tail

carnivore: an animal that eats meat

drone: any aircraft designed to fly without an onboard pilot

embryo: the developmental stage of an animal before hatching or being born

engineering: the use of science and technology to understand structures and how stresses affect them

fossil: the remains or impression of a prehistoric living thing (plant or animal) that is at least ten thousand years old. It forms when the material of the living organism is replaced by stony material or when a living thing leaves an imprint in material that becomes rock.

gastrolith: a rock or stone that an animal swallows to aid in food grinding during digestion

habitat: an animal's home environment that supplies the food, water, and shelter it needs to live and the place it can raise its young

hadrosaur: a kind of large, plant-eating dinosaur that normally walked on four legs, could possibly stand on two legs, and had a duckbill-like flat jaw

herbivore: an animal that eats plants

iguanodon: a kind of large, plant-eating dinosaur that normally walked on four legs and had back legs that were longer than its front legs

imprint fossil: a type of fossil created by something, such as a living organism, pressing into soft material and leaving an impression that hardens in the shape of what created it

laser light: a very narrow beam of one wavelength (color) of light that can be precisely aimed at a target. By comparison white light, such as light from a light bulb, is a combination of many wavelengths (colors) and spreads out in many directions.

laser-stimulated fluorescence: laser light striking a surface stimulating any chemicals embedded in the surface and causing them to glow. Laser-stimulated fluorescence has revealed never-before-seen details on imprint fossils.

lidar: using pulsed laser light to measure varying distances to Earth to produce 3D maps of Earth's surface and features on it

load sensor: an electronic device that, upon detecting compression force, automatically converts and displays it as an equivalent weight or bite force

mass spectrometer: a machine that converts material into a gas and analyzes it to determine the chemical makeup

nodosaur: an armored, plant-eating dinosaur that is a kind of ankylosaur without a club-tipped tail

paleontologist: a scientist who studies fossils, the preserved remains or imprints of living things from long ago in Earth's past

predator: an animal that lives by hunting and eating other animals

prey: an animal caught as food by another animal

sauropod: a kind of plant-eating dinosaur noted for having long necks, long tails, and four pillarlike legs

species: a kind of living thing

synchrotron: technology that accelerates charged particles (electrons), producing extremely powerful X-rays to scan things that cannot be studied with usual X-ray sources

theropod: a kind of large, meat-eating dinosaur that walked on two legs

tracksite: an area where fossilized dinosaur footprints are found

Source Notes

7 Gregory M. Erickson, telephone interview with the author, June 24, 2024.

9 Erickson.

10 Pasha van Bijlert, telephone interview with the author, August 18, 2023.

11 Van Bijlert.

12 Van Bijlert.

17 Thomas Kaye, telephone interview with the author, August 17, 2023.

20 Vincent Fernandez, telephone interview with the author, July 31, 2024.

21 Kimberley Chapelle, telephone interview with the author, August 17, 2023.

25 Eric Kappus, telephone interview with the author, August 14, 2023.

25 Eric Kappus, interview with the author, May 24, 2024.

27 Kappus.

28 Andréas Jannel, telephone interview with the author, August 21, 2023.

31 Jannel.

32 Jannel.

33 Jannel.

35 Caleb Brown, interview with the author, September 21, 2023.

36 Brown.

37 Brown.

39 Brown.

Find Out More

Check out these books and websites to discover even more:

Colson, Rob. *Dinosaur Bones: And What They Tell Us*. Firefly Books, 2016. Cleverly made to look like a paleontologist's notebook, the labeled drawings and notes let readers explore and have fun learning about prehistoric creatures, including dinosaurs.

Discovering and Investigating *Borealopelta*
https://www.youtube.com/watch?v=r3yxt-7ogso
Actual footage of discovering, revealing, and investigating one of the world's most amazingly preserved dinosaurs—*Borealopelta*.

How Dinosaur Footprints Survive 65 Million Years
https://www.youtube.com/watch?v=S-idnQZNlzE
A great look at real dinosaur tracks, the science behind their preservation through time, and a view of the world's largest sauropod footprints.

Markle, Sandra. *What If You Had T. rex Teeth: And Other Dinosaur Parts!?* Scholastic, 2019. Imagine if you had teeth or feet like a dinosaur. This picture book explores the unique features of some dinosaurs.

Rubin, Sean. *The Iguanodon's Horn: How Artists and Scientists Put a Dinosaur Back Together Again and Again and Again.* Clarion Books, 2024. A fun journey through the process that led scientists and artists to change their view of one dinosaur over time as they gained new knowledge.

T. rex Is a Slow Walker
https://www.youtube.com/watch?v=uAjfyiGFAdc
See Pasha van Bijlert's animation of *T. rex* walking.

Index

Photo Acknowledgments

Image credits: Andy Selinger/Alamy, p. 4; Kimberley Chapelle, PhD, pp. 5 (top left), 18 (top), 21 (all); Martin Shields/Alamy, pp. 5 (top right), 5 (bottom), 14; Warpaintcobra/Getty Images, pp. 6, 44 (bottom right), 45 (bottom right); Gregory M. Erickson, Ph.D., p. 7; Image designed by Paul M. Gignac with thanks to the Black Hills Institute for access to specimens, p. 8; Puwadol Jaturawutthichai/Alamy, p. 9; Tom Brown, p. 10; Pasha van Bijlert (Utrecht University/Naturalis), p. 11; CoreyFord/Getty Images, p. 12; blickwinkel/Alamy, p. 13; Tom Kaye, pp. 15 (all), 16 (all); Julius T. Csotonyi/Science Source, pp. 17, 44 (center left), 45 (top center); Mark Stevenson/Stocktrek Images/Getty Images, pp. 18 (bottom), 44 (top right), 45 (top left); aerial-photos.com/Alamy, p. 19; Jonah Choiniere / ESI, p. 20; photo taken by Farjam Ashrafzadeh of Aerial Amity LLC, pp. 22, 23, 26 (right); Arthur Dorety/Stocktrek Images/Getty Images, pp. 24–25, 44 (top left), 45 (bottom center); photo by Dean Van Matre of Great Western Land Surveying, p. 26 (left); Elenarts108/Getty Images, p. 27; Copyright Dr. Andréas Jannel, p. 29; Universal Images Group North America LLC/DeAgostini/Alamy, pp. 30, 44 (center right), 45 (bottom left); Photo by Jay P. Nair, edited by Dr. Andréas Jannel, p. 31; Jannel, A., et al. 2022 "Softening the steps to gigantism in sauropod dinosaurs through the evolution of a pedal pad." Science Advances 8.31 eabm8280. DOI: 10.1126/sciadv.abm8280, p. 32; Corey Ford/Stocktrek Images/Getty Images, p. 33; Image Courtesy of the Royal Tyrrell Museum, Drumheller, AB, pp. 34, 35, 36, 37, 38, 39, 44 (bottom left), 45 (top right); Skip Jeffery, p. 42; Ian Dagnall/Alamy, p. 43 (left); DK Photography/Alamy, p. 43 (right).

Cover: Ian Dagnall/Alamy; Arthur Dorety/Stocktrek Images/Getty Images; Adél Békefi/Getty Images; DEV IMAGES/Getty Images.